KILLER ANIMALS

GRIZZLY BEARS

ON THE HUNT

by Lori Polydoros

Reading Consultant:
Barbara J. Fox
Reading Specialist
North Carolina State University

Capstone
press

Mankato, Minnesota

Blazers is published by Capstone Press,
151 Good Counsel Drive, P.O. Box 669, Mankato, Minnesota 56002.
www.capstonepress.com

Library of Congress Cataloging-in-Publication Data
Polydoros, Lori, 1968–
    Grizzly bears: on the hunt/by Lori Polydoros.
    p. cm. — (Blazers. Killer animals)
    Includes bibliographical references and index.
    Summary: "Describes grizzly bears, their physical features, how they hunt and kill, and their
role in the ecosystem" — Provided by publisher.
    ISBN-13: 978-1-4296-2316-2 (hardcover)
    ISBN-10: 1-4296-2316-0 (hardcover)
    1. Grizzly bear — Juvenile literature. I. Title. II. Series.
QL737.C27P643 2009
599.784 — dc22   2008030566

Editorial Credits

Abby Czeskleba, editor; Kyle Grenz, designer; Wanda Winch, photo researcher

Photo Credits

AnimalsAnimals/Erwin & Peggy Bauer, 13 (inset), 21; Len Rue Jr., 18–19
Art Life Images/Mark Hamblin, cover
David A. Rein, 25
Getty Images Inc./The Image Bank/Andy Rouse, 22–23
McDonald Wildlife Photography/Joe McDonald, 17, 28–29
Minden Pictures/Konrad Wothe, 10; Michael Quinton, 26–27; Sumio Harada, 14–15;
    Yva Momatiuk & John Eastcott, 5
Peter Arnold/R. Erl, 6–7
Photo Researchers, Inc/John Shaw, 9
Shutterstock/Rick Parsons, 12–13

1 2 3 4 5 6 14 13 12 11 10 09

TABLE OF CONTENTS

ON THE HUNT

KILLER FACT

Grizzlies are a kind of brown bear.

4

Two male elk fight as their antlers crash together. A hungry grizzly bear waits in the grass nearby.

5

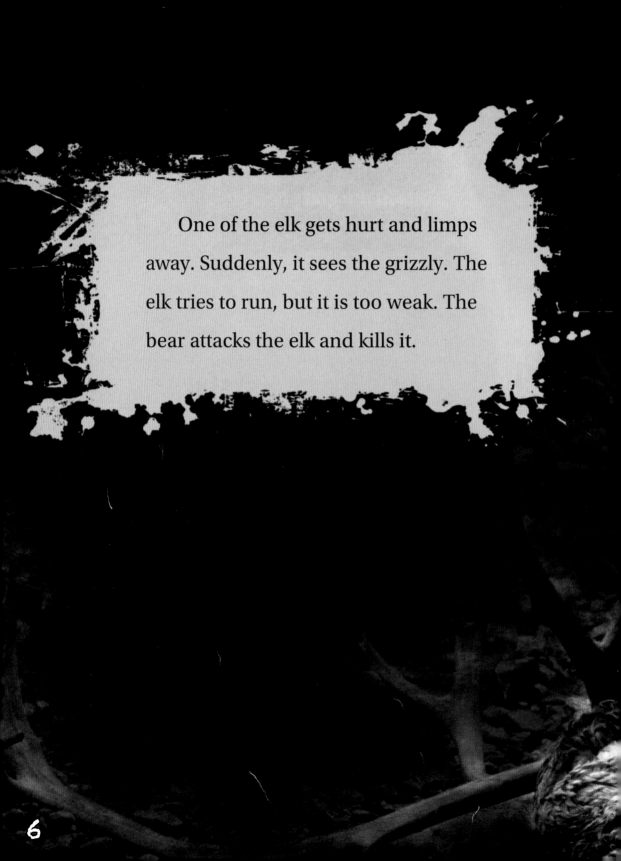

One of the elk gets hurt and limps away. Suddenly, it sees the grizzly. The elk tries to run, but it is too weak. The bear attacks the elk and kills it.

TOOLS OF THE TRADE

Grizzlies are the largest **omnivores** in North America. They weigh more than 300 pounds (136 kilograms). Grizzlies are 7 feet (2.1 meters) long. They stand 3 feet (.9 meter) tall on all fours.

omnivore – an animal that eats plants
and other animals

Grizzlies use their sharp front teeth to kill **prey**. They grind up plants with their flat back teeth.

prey – an animal hunted by another animal for food

The ground may look like it
has been plowed after a grizzly has
finished digging. Grizzlies dig up
roots with their long, sharp claws.
They also dig to find bugs.

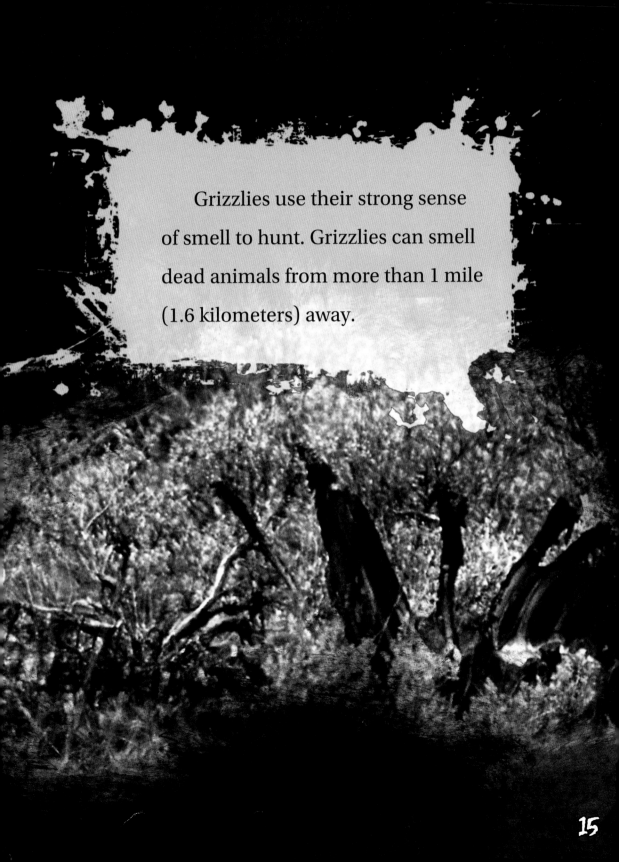

Grizzlies use their strong sense of smell to hunt. Grizzlies can smell dead animals from more than 1 mile (1.6 kilometers) away.

FIERCE HUNTERS

Grizzlies may **stalk** their prey. They can chase animals at high speeds for short distances. But most healthy animals can outrun grizzlies. Grizzlies hunt young, old, hurt, or sick animals.

stalk – to hunt an animal in a quiet, secret way

KILLER FACT

A grizzly covers leftover prey with dirt. The dirt hides the prey from other animals. The bear comes back later to eat the food.

A grizzly traps prey with its strong paws. The bear's weight and strength keep the animal from getting away.

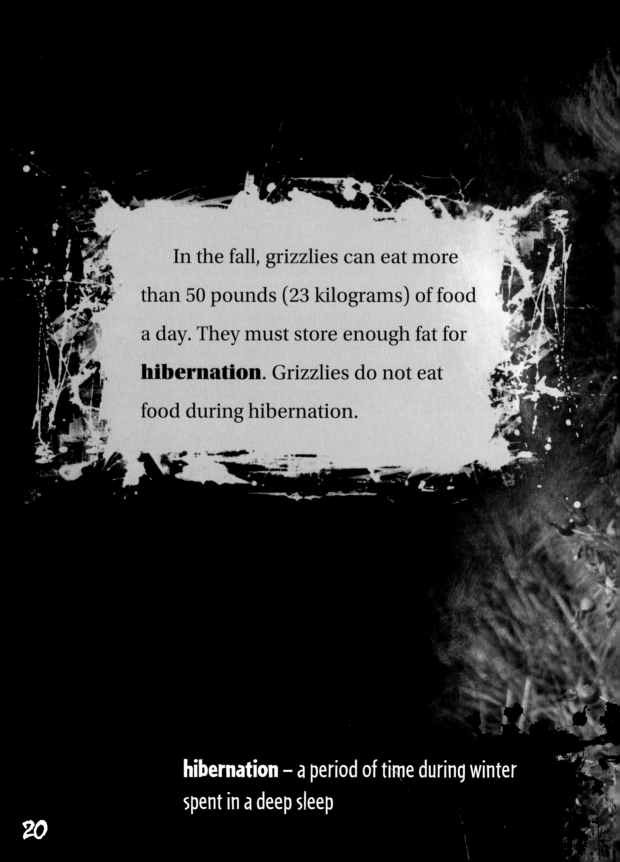

In the fall, grizzlies can eat more than 50 pounds (23 kilograms) of food a day. They must store enough fat for **hibernation**. Grizzlies do not eat food during hibernation.

hibernation – a period of time during winter spent in a deep sleep

Grizzly Bear Diagram

shoulder hump

sharp claw

large paw

strong leg

RULERS OF THE MOUNTAINS

Grizzly bears are important to the **ecosystem**. They eat plants, berries, and animals that are already dead. Eating dead animals helps lower the amount of waste.

ecosystem – a group of animals and plants that work together with their surroundings

Even though grizzlies are **dangerous** bears, they usually stay away from people. A female grizzly may attack if a person comes too close to her cubs. People must respect the rulers of the mountains.

dangerous – likely to cause harm or injury

Dinner is Served!

GLOSSARY

dangerous (DAYN-jur-uhss) — likely to cause harm or injury

ecosystem (EE-koh-sis-tuhm) — a group of animals and plants that work together with their surroundings

hibernation (hye-bur-NAY-shuhn) — a period of time during winter spent in a deep sleep

limp (LIMP) — to walk in an uneven way; an animal may limp when it is hurt.

omnivore (OM-nuh-vor) — an animal that eats plants and other animals

prey (PRAY) — an animal hunted by another animal for food

stalk (STAWK) — to hunt an animal in a quiet, secret way

READ MORE

Sartore, Joel. *Face to Face with Grizzlies.* Face to Face. Washington, D.C.: National Geographic, 2007.

Stevens, Kathryn. *Grizzly Bears.* New Naturebooks. Mankato, Minn.: Child's World, 2008.

Thomas, Isabel. *Polar Bear vs. Grizzly Bear.* Animals Head to Head. Chicago: Raintree, 2006.

INTERNET SITES

FactHound offers a safe, fun way to find educator-approved Internet sites related to this book.

Here's what you do:

1. Visit *www.facthound.com*
2. Choose your grade level.
3. Begin your search.

This book's ID number is 9781429623162.

FactHound will fetch the best sites for you!

INDEX